Fun at the Beach

Julie A. Walker

AuthorHouse™
1663 Liberty Drive
Bloomington, IN 47403
www.authorhouse.com
Phone: 1-800-839-8640

First published by AuthorHouse 9/6/2011

ISBN: 978-1-4567-5926-1 (sc)

Library of Congress Control Number: 2011907552

Printed in the United States of America

Any people depicted in stock imagery provided by Thinkstock are models,
and such images are being used for illustrative purposes only.
Certain stock imagery © Thinkstock.

This book is printed on acid-free paper.

"Thank-you to my family members who lent me their artistic talents; Mom (sunset pg. 22-23), Cooper (crab, pg. 12), Colton (crab,
pg. 12), Scott (ear, pg. 14), and Anna who spotted the missing hair! Your interest and support means so much to me."

authorHOUSE®

This book is dedicated to Grandma, for her beach at the ocean, and Grandpa, for his beach at the lake. Fun times and fond memories to last a lifetime. Thank-you, we love you!

There are many different beaches around the world.
Some are by the ocean and others by a lake.

Finding things to do at a beach is easy, we can play in the sand, go swimming, collect shells, and just have fun! My name is Cooper, my sister is Anna, and we love to go to the beach with our family to play all day!

My dad helps me fly a kite on a windy
day at the beach.

My grandma lives by a beach on the ocean. An ocean has salty water. I like it when Grandma helps me find coquina shells down by the shore. They poke out and then wiggle back into the sand when the water uncovers them. The shells are tiny and all different colors. Some are white, blue, pink, yellow, purple, or orange.

Grandma and I love to swim in the ocean and float over the waves. Salt water makes it easier for us to float!

My grandpa lives in a house at a lake. A lake is made of fresh water. Grandpa loves to help us build things in the sand. Look at the big alligator we made this time.

Sometimes Anna and I make a house out of sand at the beach with our cousin. We dig a big hole and then build the different rooms. Can you find the kitchen? How about the bathroom and family room?

Anna likes me to bury her in the sand so that only her head and shoulders are showing. It is a lot of shoveling but a lot of fun!

We then need a snack and a cold drink. It's fun to have a picnic on the beach. Just watch out for the seagulls, they like a snack too!

Anna loves to run fast and chase the seagulls down the beach. They fly away and then come right back. I think they like this game just as much as Anna likes it!

It is also fun to play frisbee or catch with a ball. There are so many games you can play at the beach.

It is nice to go for a walk with my mom and collect pretty seashells in our buckets. We can make crafts with them later.

At the end of the day we sit and watch the sunset. What fun we have had at the beach.

Cooper and Anna

Bye for now! Join us again soon as we
do and see more fun things.

CPSIA information can be obtained
at www.ICGtesting.com
Printed in the USA
LVHW02n0043250118
563900LV00002B/6/P